OPEN SAYS ME!

<u>THE</u> SYSTEM THAT CAN OPEN ANY AND ALL OPPORTUNITIES IN YOUR CAREER

CARLOS V. DAVIS

ISBN: 1503000583
ISBN-13: 978-1503000582

DEDICATION

To April, Jordan, Seth, my parents O'Dean and Fely Davis, my Shreveport family, my Arkansas family(Little Rock and NWA), my Los Angeles family, my Seattle family, my Charlotte family, and any and all who I have served and will serve!

CONTENTS

PREFACE

I know that the preface is the most skipped part of any book. I know you want to get to the MEAT and POTATOES of this book to become a MASTER networker, but you have to get the foundation of where this book got its start. Just bear with me, and I promise that this part of the book will be just as valuable as the other parts of this book.

Professional networking is not a new concept. Even before the dawn of the American society, networking has been used to grow businesses, religions, and organizations. But, with the dawn of industry and technology, professional networking became one of those forgotten professional skills. It has even gotten a bad rap in business, as it was a tactic in building illegal pyramid schemes. When I graduated from college back in 2001, I had no idea what networking was, nor did I know that I needed to know how to do it. It wasn't until I started my IT job that a mentor of mine mentioned that I needed to network to grow my career. My thoughts were, 'Networking? What is that?' I didn't think I needed to do it, so I didn't. When I started my entrepreneurial ventures, my mentors told me the same thing! There was no elective or class that taught professional networking in my high school or college nor did anyone give me any advice on it, so I was shocked that people around me were emphasizing that I needed to know this skill. When my career and business went nowhere, I eventually gave in and decided to learn how to network. I started asking around for advice on how to network. The problem was that everyone's advice was different. I didn't want to be closed-minded to the advice, so I took everything in. One bit of advice that I got that made sense was that all the networking I needed to do was on the internet. Hearing that, I dedicated all of my time to being in front of my computer. Keep in mind this was before the dawn of social media, so all of the networking I did was done via chat rooms and lead generation sites. After spending numerous hours and days online looking for career and business leads and not getting any results, I came to the conclusion that this was not the way to go. Another bit of advice I got was to go to networking events. I was open to the advice, but here was my issue: What do I do and what do I say? I asked around on what to do, and one colleague said to just pass out a whole bunch of business cards so everyone knows who you are. So, I went from networking event to networking event and passed out as many business cards as I could, and after every event, I went home and waited for someone to call me. Sadly, no one called me. I started to get frustrated and decided to put matters in my own hands and do what I felt would get me results!

Before I move on with my story, have you ever run into one of those so-called networkers who's always 'vomiting?' I know that's a bit graphic, but let me give you more details. You've probably run into a vomiter at your local shopping mall, grocery store, discount retailer, or even at your place of worship! You will see him (or her) lurking about in the shadows, behind bushes, fountains, or racks of merchandise. Once you've made eye contact with a 'vomiter,' WATCH OUT!! You have now become their prey!! They walk up to you with a big huge smile, and then…HERE COMES THE VOMIT!! They begin rattling off what they are trying to sell, what you should invest in, about how they have a great vacation deal if you hear a presentation, and many, MANY other things that you may or may not care about. The biggest sign that you are talking to a vomiter is that they do not once try to get to know who you are. All they care to do is TELL you why you should know them, why you should buy what they have, and/or why you should hire them. Now, vomiters are not just found in where you may do your shopping. Vomiters will also frequent networking events, business expos, and other events where business people may congregate. When I go to networking events, I can always tell when vomiters are there. I have been networking for several years, and I can sit back and point out the vomiters. There was one guy who was a KNOWN vomiter who would be at almost every networking event that I was at. When people saw him coming, they would run the other way!! He would go from person to person to person with his 'pitch' and his ego. I felt sorry for the people who congregated in a corner, because if he got someone in the corner, he would talk them into submission!! What was sad was that after he talked to someone, the person would have the most sour and disgusted look on their face as if he had actually vomited all over his or her shirt! It didn't help that he was a jerk also. Some vomiters are jerks; some are not. In either case, they leave the person they were talking to with the feeling that they just wanted to 'sell' them something and they cared nothing about who they were. Here is the really sad part:

THAT PERSON WAS ME!!

Before I became a master networker, I was that guy! And to make matters worse, I taught my marketing team for my business to be vomiters also. We would plan our days around where we would go and how many people we were going to 'talk' to. Yes, we hid behind the bushes and merchandise racks waiting for our next victim, er, sale! We would look for the sharpest dressed people, folks with kids, and anything that had a pulse to talk to. Our day was not completed until we talked, er, vomited on 10 - 20 people. Did we care about what they did? Heck no! Did we care what their dreams were? Absolutely not! All we cared about was making sure they knew about our company, our service, and why we were the best thing in the world! Now, why did we do all of this? Because, we didn't know any better! All I did was what I THOUGHT was right and copy what others who I thought knew how to network do, and in turn, I taught it to my sales team. I noticed that our sales numbers started to decline, but I said to myself, "Hey, this is a numbers game, so we just need to talk to MORE PEOPLE!" And that is what my sales team and I did. We went out and vomited on more people.

And here is when the revelation came:

I remember being at a networking event, and as soon as I entered the room, I started to get sour looks from people. As I started walking towards people I knew, they started conversations with other people. I thought, "What's wrong with them?" I didn't realize at the time the problem wasn't them; the problem was with me. It wasn't until I started talking to a close friend of mine that I realized what I had become. I asked my friend in an arrogant tone, "What is wrong with everyone?? It's like no one wants to talk to me!" My colleague said, "They don't. They heard about you from some people that you have done business with, and they really don't want to deal with you." At first I was furious! I said to myself, "How dare they! They don't know what they're missing out on!!" I then remembered the sales numbers still going down after the decision to talk to more people. I also started thinking about the people I talked to and the fact that I knew NOTHING about them. I went from being angry to sad. Because I was so focused on the numbers and the dollar signs, I had bypassed numerous opportunities to get to know the people I was talking to. I left that networking event and I realized that the people at that event didn't want to talk to me because of the reputation I had created for myself.

From that point, I decided to change my whole approach to doing business. I became a student of true networking and building relationships. I sought out the experts in proper professional networking and business building and learned the correct attitudes and philosophies about the subject. A lot of my habits were hard to break. Once they were broken, perceptions about me changed, and my income and career changed for the better. By learning and implementing the right way to network, I have gained opportunities in radio, legal service brokering, and now professional development.

My reason for writing this book is to help you be a better networker and a better relationship builder. In this day and age, cash is still king, but one bit of currency that is on the rise is what is called social capital. What is social capital? It's a sociology term stating that it is the expected collective or economic benefits derived from the cooperation between individuals and groups. With the world being connected now more than ever, there is a high value of having a great network of people at your disposal. Over the past several years, I have learned some great techniques to help you not only increase your business and career opportunities, but most importantly, improve the relationships around you. You don't have to be in the business world to be a better networker or relationship builder. If you want to just build better relationships in general, this book will help you AND the people around you. If you know your networking skills are not correct, I hope you can relate to my story and see how you can improve. I have walked in your shoes, so I know what you go through every day. My intent is to help you make the same realization and improvements that I did.

Regardless of where you are in your life, you have to work this book. In order for this book to work for you, you first have to make a decision that you want to change and improve. If you don't make that decision, then nothing that I teach you in this book will work or be of any worth to you. Do you remember the movie The Matrix? I am a geek at heart, and it is one of my favorite movies of all time. For those of you who lived under a rock in the early 2000s, the movie is about a young man named Neo (played by Keanu Reeves) learning about the reality that he was living in a computer-generated world. There is a scene where he is introduced to Morpheus (played by Lawrence Fishburne) and Morpheus is educating him on what the Matrix is. After Morpheus gives Neo a brief description of what is going on, Neo is still hesitant about believing what Morpheus is telling him. It's at that point that Morpheus delivers one of the most memorable lines in the movie: "After this there is no turning back. You take the blue pill: the story ends, you wake up in your bed, and you believe what you want to believe; you take the red pill: you stay in Wonderland and I show you how far the rabbit hole goes..." I ask the same question of you. Do you take the red pill or the blue pill?

BLUE PILL – CLOSE THE BOOK AND PUT THE BOOK DOWN

RED PILL – TURN TO THE NEXT PAGE

1 THE FOUNDATION

Welcome to your networking journey! I am so honored and glad you decided to go down the road of improving your networking skills. I promise you won't be disappointed in the knowledge and experience you will receive. We'll start with the foundations of networking. Networking is a lot like building a house: you have to start with a plan and a firm foundation. Actually, you have to have these two items in a lot of areas in life, but having a plan and a foundation for your networking is very important, even before you begin your quest in becoming a better networker. I know you're thinking:

"Oh great…more setup stuff before we get to the 'real' knowledge…"

You may think having a foundation is not important, but it is quite crucial. Think about a house that is being built. Before the roof is put on and before the walls are put up, you have to have a plan and you have to have a foundation. Networking is not just something you pick up. Just ask the many vomiters who have crossed your path in the last few months! Those individuals just get up, get out, and start spewing!! Networking is an art and a process, and in order to start down the path of being better you have to have a great foundation. This chapter will focus on your intentions for networking and the results you want to achieve with networking. Harvey MacKay is quoted to saying "If you fail to plan, you plan to fail." To help you with developing your intentions and goals, I have prepared a self-evaluation sheet for you to download. The best part about it is that it is ABSOLUTELY FREE!!

Just go to http://www.facebook.com/istandanddeliver, and post on the wall that you would like the evaluation sheet. Feel free to send me an Inbox message if you don't want to post on the wall of the page. If you LIKE the page and you own a business, let me know, and I'll be sure to promote your business by letting our followers know you stopped by. There are also other FREE goodies I am offering that I will be referencing later!

As you would take your job or your business seriously, I would like you to take this portion of the process seriously as well. Just as high school, college, and even the military (Thank you to those who serve, by the way!) prepares you for the later stages in life, this part of the book will prepare you for what you will encounter when you are out networking. I can remember playing football and basketball, and there was always one drill that I HATED! In basketball, I could not stand doing the rebound drills! I played Point Guard and Shooting Guard, so since I wasn't the biggest guy on the court, I didn't think the skill was needed. Day in and day out, I suffered through this drill. One day, I asked my coach, "As a guard, why in the world do I have to do this drill?!" He took his whistle out of mouth, put his hand on my shoulder, and said, "Preparation..." He put his whistle back in his mouth, and he didn't say anything else about it! I had the most puzzled look on my face after that! I shrugged my shoulders, and kept pressing on. It wasn't until the season started that what he said made sense. It was in the game situation when all of those drills came in handy. There were numerous situations when I was matched up with another guard, and I was able to out-rebound my opponent. After the first game, I told my coach, "Thank you..." and he knew what I was talking about.

Developing your "why"

So, my first question to you is, why do you want to be a better networker? Is it that you are a sales person and you want more clients? Are you a small business owner looking for some potential new hires to staff it? Are you looking for a new career or occupation? While these are definitely good reasons to be a better networker, I want you to dig deeper as to why you want to be a better networker. I want you to look into your heart and really look at why you want to be a better networker. A mentor told me a long time ago that your "why" has to be strong enough to make you cry and help you get past any negative situation that you may face. The reason 'the why' has to be this strong is to prevent you from quitting. Because this step is so important, I suggest you take about 15 - 30 minutes to yourself away from your daily distractions to develop this. This can be your favorite getaway place or it could be just you going to your favorite room in your home.

Regardless of where you go, you will need to be in a place of peace and quiet to develop this.

I remember when I created the 'why' for my legal services brokerage business. At the time, I was working for a major retail corporation in their Information Systems area. I was making good money, but the corporate environment was not sitting well with me. A couple of my coworkers came to me saying that they were in the process of building a record company, and they needed some help. I'll never forget the first thing I said: "Um, I've never helped run and build a record company." One of my partners said, "That's ok...We've never done it either!" We did very well, and the reason why we did well is because we had a strong desire to be successful. No matter what adversity we faced, we were determined to be a success. From there, I transitioned into the event planning industry and finally into the legal services business. Before I got started in my legal services business, my business mentor told me to write down why I was doing this business. I looked at him and said, "Are you serious?? I am a successful businessman, so I don't feel I need to do this." I was very hesitant at first, but I did it. Here is what I wrote down:

To retire early
To make a lot of money
To have time freedom

I know these things may seem shallow, but it's why I was doing the business. From there, my mentor asked me why I wanted those things. I went on to tell him about my troubles within my current job. I talked about how I was working very long hours and not making the kind of money I should have been making in the Information Technology industry. I told him that no matter how hard I worked, I was not moving up within the company. I was overlooked for numerous promotions, and I was not living the life that I felt I should be living. After going over my troubles, I remember how angry I was, and it actually brought a tear to my eye. My mentor then said, "Now, THAT is your why!!" Keep in mind that 'why' was created when I was single and I was seven years into my career. Since then, I have gotten married and had two sons, so my 'why' has expanded to include giving the best to my wife and children.

As you go to your quiet place, begin thinking about your own life and what you would like to improve. You may be in the same position I was in when I first created my first 'why' or you may be in a totally different part of your life. Regardless of what's going on in your life, make that the focus point of 'why' you want to be a better networker. Your 'why' can be one statement or it can be several. What's important is making sure that it moves you and creates a 'no quit' attitude. After you write it out, read it to yourself a few times and think about a troubling time in your life. If your 'why' does not push you to get past that difficult time, then rewrite your why. Remember, you why has to stir you up emotionally. You will see a place on your worksheet to write down your 'final' why, but your 'why' will never be final. As you go and grow in life, your 'why' will evolve as you do, so you will need to take time to rewrite your 'why' once a year. I would recommend detaching your 'why' from your worksheet. Why? (I know, I know...It's a lot of 'whys'!) This is so you can place it somewhere that you frequent like your desk or your bathroom sink to look at it multiple times throughout the day. This will serve as daily inspiration. Next, we will look at your clients or who you are serving.

Your potential clients

Who are you selling to or who do you want to hire you? In the client section of the evaluation, you will see this question. PLEASE DO NOT WRITE DOWN EVERYONE!! While we all think that we have a product, service, or skill that EVERYONE needs, the product, service, or skill we offer does better in some demographics than others. While some industries can overlap with who they serve, I want you to determine who you best serve. What do I mean? I want you to do a detailed evaluation of the market segments you service. Some of you may be saying to yourself,

"This sounds like a marketing class! I didn't get this book for marketing; I got this book to be a better networker!!"

Before you close this book and try to get a refund (if you have the e-book version, you are stuck!), knowing your market is very important in your networking efforts. Why? The more you know about your client, the easier it will be for you to connect with them and the easier it will be for you to do business with them, even if it's for hiring purposes. This will also make it easier for you to get referrals from them, and more than likely those referrals will be very similar to them. Remember, birds of a feather flock together!

If you are looking at the 'Who are you selling to?' question in the evaluation, you will see the different demographics underneath it. I will go over each demographic very briefly to assist you in filling out this section of the evaluation. If you are a new business and/or you have never been in your respective industry, you may want to do some research online to get a little insight on the demographics of your industry. If you are job hunting, some of this will apply and some won't. If you are a marketing expert, please bear with me:

Gender

This is pretty self-explanatory. Does your product/service serve males, females, or both better? If you sell make-up, then the answer is pretty obvious (unless you're a guy who's into that type of stuff!). If you feel that your product/service serves both genders, put the percentage that you feel your product/service serves each gender. For example, if you're a company that sells lawn mowers, you might put 70% for males and 30% for females. Traditionally, males do more lawn mowing, but I know several females who mow lawns, especially if they have a riding mower!

Age

This is a very broad category, and one of the more difficult to narrow down. It's best to give a range of age or ages that you can serve. For example, if you were a life insurance agent, you would be better to serve the 30 - 60 age range versus the 18 - 22 age range. On the flip side, you would better serve the 18 - 22 age range if you were a trendy clothing store. Again, this is a broad category, so do your best with determining the range.

Income range

This is asking what range your client's yearly income falls into. This is also a broad category, but it helps to get the right range. If you are a real estate agent who focuses on luxury homes, you will not focus on a person who makes $40,000 a year. If you were an agent who focused on modest priced homes, this person will be better suited for you. Knowing this is very important, as you want to make sure that the price point of your product(s)/service(s) matches who you are trying to get in front of.

Marital status

Like gender, this is pretty self-explanatory. When filling this out, do like you did gender and put percentages next to the statuses that you serve.

Geographic location

Now, you're probably thinking,

"Um, I am just going to be networking with folks in my city, so why in the heck is this important??!!!"

Back in the day, this would not matter unless you did a lot of traveling, but with the world becoming smaller due to the internet and social media, knowing this demographic is very important. Knowing what geographic location(s) your product(s)/service(s) will serve is imperative in having the multi-channel networking system work for you. Networking and building a successful career is not just about knowing the right folks in your backyard. If you are serious about your career growing, you always have to be thinking about expansion into other marketplaces. This is especially true if you are looking for employment as you may need to find a job in your industry in a different city and/or state.

Who are they currently buying from/Who are they hiring?

You're probably saying to yourself, "They need to be buying from/hiring ME!"

While I agree with you, you need to know who your competition is. Why is this important? You need to learn why they are currently buying from your competitors or hiring others. It is also important to know why people DO NOT buy from your competitors or hire them. This knowledge will help you in the YOU section of the multi-channel program in this book. The more you know about your competition, the better you can compete in the marketplace. Even though you may have some 'new, never seen, groundbreaking' product/service/skill, you have some type of competition. There are no new industries out there, and whatever you are offering falls into one of them. Again, we will go into more detail about this in the YOU section.

Just like you did for the 'Why?' section of the evaluation, go to your 'quiet' place to concentrate and focus on each demographic. I cannot tell you how many 'vomiters' I have seen who try to sell to any and everybody!! I can remember being at a networking event where this happened to my wife. At this event, there was a group of individuals promoting their 'body slimming' girdles. While I was speaking with someone, I noticed that one of the 'body slimming' guys walked up to my wife saying that their girdle was something she really needed. Let me describe my wife to you in two words: PETITE and FIT! This product was something that my wife definitely DID NOT need, but this guy really felt that she needed to purchase this from him. In fact, my wife felt a bit offended by his approach and asked him quite bluntly, "Do you think I'm fat???!!!" Of course, the guy had to backtrack and try to explain himself. By then it was too late, and my wife had walked away. What did he do next? You guessed it! He made his way towards me. I said to myself, "Great...let me get a towel to clean up the vomit he is about to spew..." I guess he thought that by talking to me, I could help him sell to my wife. After his ten minute 'presentation' about why he felt she needed it (along with another 2 minutes of why I needed it and needed to help him sell it!!), I politely took myself away from the conversation. Like I said before, the more you know about your client, the better your chances of getting that client's business and that client's referrals, so do not take this section lightly.

The goals of your networking

Some of you are probably asking,

"Wait a minute...I thought we already did this?! Aren't the goals and why I am doing this the same???"

Not necessarily. Your 'Why' is the REASON you are networking; your goals are the RESULTS of your networking. You will want your goals to be VERY specific, as this will give you something to shoot for every day. Here are some of my goals when I go network:

Attend 2 - 3 networking events a week
Meet 10 - 20 people at the event
Connect 5 - 10 of those people to the resources that they are needing
Have 5 of those individuals become clients

These aren't all of my goals, but just a few to give you an idea of what I set out to do when I plan my week of networking. Keep in mind, my goals don't revolve around specific events. My goals revolve around what I plan to do in a period of time. Your goals will not be the same as mine, as our reasons and industries are different, but be sure to take some time to write them out and put them somewhere where you can see them often. This will allow you to stay on track each day, week, etc. on how you are doing towards them. I would also advise having a place to write down what you actually do each day, week, etc. versus your goals. This will help you in being accountable to how you are working towards your goals. It's also good to have an accountability partner in your networking. Start to think about the individual(s) in your life who you feel can keep you focused on your goals.

Now that we have gotten the preparation out of the way, it's time to set up our MULTI-CHANNEL networking experience.

MULTI-CHANNEL WHAT?

Now before you go asking your cable/satellite service provider for this, it has nothing to do with what you watch on TV; it has EVERYTHING to do with how you network and communicate with your potential and current clients. What do I mean by multi-channel? It's very simple, and I can sum it up in one word. Ready? Here we go:

ADVERTISING

Now I know the majority of you reading this are ready to throw this book out of the window. (If you have a Kindle, iPad, or E-reader, please think twice before you pitch it out the window.) You are probably saying:

"Is that it??!!!" "I spent my hard earned money on this??"

I wouldn't be surprised if a few expletives are coming out of your mouth. Before you decide to close the book, let me explain what I mean.

A major company has a product(s)/service(s) that they want to sell to their consumer base. In order to sell said product(s)/service(s), the company has to let their consumer base know that their product(s)/service(s) exist. How do they do this? They advertise. When they advertise they use multiple media outlets or 'channels' to get in front of their consumer base. Some of the most popular and effective channels are television, radio, billboards, and print. Some other channels include sponsoring events and commercial real estate (Bank of America Stadium, Amway Arena, etc.). Because a major company has a MAJOR advertising budget, they can use any and all of these channels to get in front of their consumer base.

Now, let's look at YOUR company/business/brand. I can make the obvious assumption that you do not have the same advertising budget as a company like Nike or Microsoft. If you did, you would not need this book! Although you don't have their advertising dollars, you have the ability to set up a multi-channel system! You won't be able to utilize TV, radio, and print like the big boys, but you will be able to utilize two channels that the big companies are using to help them beat their competition: BRANDING and SOCIAL MEDIA.

One marketing strategy that is old as the beginning of time is word of mouth advertising. While it's the oldest, companies of all sizes still consider it the most effective. If used properly, it can propel your business to the highest of heights, but if not used properly, it can hurt your business. With the birth of social media, word of mouth has gone from local to global, and you have the opportunity to advertise and network on a worldwide stage! Because of the success of Facebook and Twitter, large corporations have made a conscious effort to make sure that social media is part of their advertising strategy. While your advertising and marketing budget may be small, you can still set up an AFFORDABLE yet EFFECTIVE Multi-Channel Networking System to reach your core 'customers' who you described in this chapter. Here is what is involved in the Multi-Channel Networking System:

YOU and YOUR BRAND
Facebook
Twitter
LinkedIn

The purpose of each channel is to do the following:

Serve as an entry point for new prospects
Serve as 'follow up' points for new prospects and current clients
Drive the prospect to your 'Point of Sale' (If you are job hunting, your point of sale will be you getting to a job interview)
Drive the prospect to bring referrals into the system

While this system is affordable, it will cost you a few things:

A little bit of money: There are a few things in this system that will cost a little money, but I promise it won't cost an 'arm and a leg.' If you are a job seeker, a website will not be needed, but if you are a business owner, I would highly recommend investing in a website for branding and point of sale purposes if you have not already set this up. There are some other things you will purchase, and I will talk about those in a later chapter. Again, my goal is to SAVE YOU MONEY!!

Time and COMMITMENT: While social media accounts are free, they and the other components of the MULTI-CHANNEL networking system take time to set up, implement, and maintain. In order for the system to work you have to be committed to the system. I will show you how to put some parts of the system on 'auto-pilot,' but you will need to be committed to monitoring the results to make sure you are maximizing the system.

2 FIRST CHANNEL - YOU

This is the channel I will spend the most time on because it is truly THE MOST IMPORTANT CHANNEL in the area of professional networking. You could have the best looking website, a top notch résumé, and thousands of Facebook and Twitter followers, but if your brand is not where it needs to be, then the other channels will not work. Think of your brand as the 'centerpiece' for all of the other channels. Remember, anyone can enter your system from any of the channels, but it is you and your brand that affects how the other channels work. It's a lot like meeting a 'fake' person. What is a 'fake' person you ask? It is someone who talks and acts one way, but that is not who they truly are as a person. The same rule applies with the channels. Your channels need to reflect who you are as a person and your values. If they don't, the people who meet you will find out that you are not who you say or appear to be.

"Well, what is my brand?"

Great question! I have created an exercise that will help you determine what you brand is. Just like the 'why' exercise, visit the Stand & Deliver Facebook page, let me know you would like to use it, and I'll let you download it at NO COST! Just like when you created your why, take some 'quiet' time to do this as you will need to concentrate on determining your brand. Once your brand is determined, the rest of the tools we will talk about will be easy to develop and maintain. These tools will be vital in your networking efforts, as they will be extensions of you and your brand. Most importantly, they will lead the people who you meet to each of the channels of your networking system. Because of this, it is important that each tool be set up properly to ensure that your networking efforts are successful. You may be asking and saying,

"What's the big deal with having proper tools?! As long as I am out networking I will be fine!"

Let's say you wanted to go fishing. If you wanted to go salt water fishing to fish for marlin, you wouldn't use the same rod, reel, and bait that you would use to go catch catfish, would you? Even the type of boat and where you would fish would be different! Professional networking is no different than fishing. Every networking environment is different, so it is imperative that you have the right tools at your disposal. Each of the following tools will be explained in detail: business card, elevator speech, and list of resources.

Business Card

I want you to take a quick glance at the three business cards on the next page.

Out of the three, which of these is the most memorable? Although this book is in black and white, most people I have surveyed chose #2. What makes the card stand out is the person's photo on the card. The purpose of the card is not just to pass along information about you, your company, etc. The TRUE purpose of the card is so people can relate YOU to what you do. We are visual people, so a picture added to your business card will increase the odds of the other person remembering you and relating you to what you do. This is especially important when you are trying to separate yourself from your competition. Did you notice that all three cards deal with people in the real estate business? What set #2 apart from the others was not the company and not the logo. The photo made all of the difference. If you work for someone, they may have already set standards for your business cards, but if they are open to allowing you to have your picture on the card, I would encourage you to have it added. Now, you can't have just any old picture on your card. Take a look at the next two business cards:

What perceptions do you get from card #1 versus card #2? Card #2 seems more 'professional' than card #1, right? Remember, image is EVERYTHING, even with a business card! You could dress well and speak well, but your business card is going to be the reference point to 'remind' the person of who you are. If your business card is unprofessional in appearance and setup, then that is the perception the person will have of you. It doesn't sound fair, but that is how we are as human beings. Now, there is A LOT of information you can put on a business card, but you want to make sure you put just enough to make you memorable and have the person want to have a meeting with you. Here are a few other items to make your business card memorable:

- Professional address

If you're working for someone, more than likely your company's address is on your business card. If you are an entrepreneur or consultant who works from home, I would encourage leasing a P.O. Box. Not only will this enhance the professional look of your business, it will add a safety measure. We live in a time where identity theft is at an all-time high. To protect you and your family, it's always best to put a professional address on your card or no address at all.

- Website

This allows the person to do some 'homework' on you and/or your company on their own time. If you work for someone, they will provide which website(s) to have on your card. If you do not have a website and you are a business owner, I strongly recommend investing in one. There are numerous online services that can help you create a website. Depending on your budget, I recommend working with a webmaster to help personalize your site based on your company and needs. You can go to sites like www.elance.com or www.thumbtack.com to find one in your budget. You can also network to find one using the skills and system in this book and make them a part of your 'success team.' The 'success team' will be discussed later.

- QR code

Have you looked at someone else's card or a poster in your favorite store and noticed one of those funky looking pictures that they want you to scan with your smartphone? That is a QR code. A QR code is a personalized code that brings up your website, email address, or whatever you have linked to it when it is scanned with a smartphone. It is a technology that has revolutionized how quickly information is received, as it allows information to be brought up on the spot versus waiting until someone gets in front of a computer. If you work for a company, they may or may not have this available for your business card. If you work for yourself, there are many sites online that can set one up for you so you can place it on your business card. A QR code is an added bonus, but it's not mandatory to have. If it's not in your budget to get one, I wouldn't break the bank to get one. I would rather you spend your money on your website and other pieces of the multi-channel system versus something like this.

- Social media information

Your social media sites are other entry points into your networking system, so it is vital to have one or more on your card. Each type of social media has it's own chapter in this book, and I'll go over each in detail. Make sure that the social media that you put on your card is professional and reflects your business and not your personal life. If you work for someone, they probably have someone maintaining the social media sites for the company, so it will be up to them whether or not they want their social media sites on your card.

- Email address

I've been around long enough to remember when email addresses first started showing up on business cards. It was the 'hot new thing' at the time, and everyone had to make sure they had their email address on their business card. Although social media is now the 'big thing,' an email address is still a vital part of the business card. A lot of people have not transitioned into social media for communication purposes, so an email address is needed as much as a phone number, especially now that people get email on their phones. If you're an entrepreneur, make sure that your email address reflects your brand and business. If your current email address is lovemachine1942@hotmail.com, you probably want to use a different email for folks to contact you about your business. While the use of Gmail, Yahoo, and Hotmail accounts have become more acceptable in the business world, it's always good to use an email address associated with your website as it will bring an added level of professionalism.

'Elevator Speech'

When you are approached by 'vomiters,' they normally will try to tell you any and everything about their company and their 'deal.' Because of this, the person they are talking to will not only not gain any interest in what is said, but they won't be able to pinpoint any value that is offered. Instead of trying to give a lot of information at one time, it's always good to have an elevator speech handy. An elevator speech is a brief statement that describes your career or business. An elevator speech can be composed in various ways. Regardless of how it is set up, it needs to do the following: introduce, inform, and intrigue. It also needs to be very short in length. All of the best elevator speeches that I have heard always had all of those three components, and they didn't take long to deliver. Here is an example of an elevator speech I used for one of my businesses:

Let me ask you a question: "If you could pick up the phone, talk to an attorney, get great advice, but not have to pay the bill, would you do it?"

It's short, it introduces a little of what my company does, and it is intriguing enough for people to want to know more about what we do. I can't tell you how many business appointments I have set just from giving this elevator speech. I will talk about the importance of setting up a meeting or appointment later in this chapter, and the elevator speech is essential in whether or not the appointment is set. I have a FREE elevator speech exercise to help you create your elevator speech, so visit http://www.facebook.com/istandanddeliver and let me know if you want a copy. If you already have one and want to improve it, the exercise will help you do that as well.

List of personal resources aka 'Your Success Team'

You're probably asking yourself, "What in the world does a list of resources have to do with networking?!"

The answer: Everything! You may think that everyone needs your product or service every time you present it to someone, but in reality, that is not true. It may be true that they need it, but they may not need it at the time you meet them.

"Well, what does that have to do with a list of resources?"

Great question! Remember, networking is all about finding out the needs of others (not your needs!) and fulfilling them. You can't do everything, so if you meet someone who needs something you don't offer, why not refer him/her to someone who does? This is your 'success team'!

"But, that means I am losing a customer and giving that customer to someone else?!"

On the contrary, you are GAINING a future customer and future referrals! Many so-called networkers are only in it for themselves and what they can gain. The ones who are willing to refer others and be a resource provider are the ones who end up very successful.

Let's say you are a plumber, and the person you are meeting is in dire need of an electrician as the lights in his home just went out due to bad wiring. You just happen to have a friend who is an electrician who does amazing work. When you pass that referral on to that person a couple of things happen:

1. *The person you are networking with gets what he/she is in need of* - This is the most obvious, but it is the most important. Regardless of whether the need is severe or not, you have just shown the person that you are a person who cares.

2. *The person will become a future customer AND referrer of business* - Because of your act of kindness, you have now become memorable! The person will not only remember your kindness, you will be the first person he or she thinks about when what you offer becomes a need or want. That person will also remember you when the people that he/she knows need your product/services, and he/she will very likely recommend you to his/her network!

3. *The person you recommended will refer business AND become a customer* - Just like the person you gave the recommendation to, the person you recommended will appreciate your act and remember you. They will be more than happy to send referrals your way, and if they are not already a customer, they will ultimately become one!

This is why having a **good** list of resources is essential. I have the word good bolded, because the resources that you refer others to must be good if not great. If not, the opposite of the above will occur. Let's say the same scenario above occurs but the electrician never returns their phone call or, worse yet, gives them the worst service imaginable. You can almost guarantee that you will be seen in the same bad light as the bad electrician you recommended. It's the law of association. Just as you take the hiring of the right staff seriously, who you chose to refer business to needs to be taken just as seriously. Go to http://www.facebook.com/istandanddeliver and let us know you want the free referral exercise to create your master referral list. If you already have a referral list, I still encourage you to do the exercise to make sure have the right folks on your 'team.'

How one enters this channel

A person enters this channel by encountering YOU. This means that you have to be ready and 'on' at all times, as you never know who you could be meeting. Your brand has to be on display at all times. Regardless of whether you are at a chamber event or at the grocery store, you have to be ready. A lot of people ask me, "Do you wear a suit everywhere you go?" I had a good friend of mine joke with someone and say, "Carlos wears a suit to bed and when he cuts his grass!" I will be honest and transparent. I wear a suit about 80% of the time. Why? That's MY brand. I am BIG on professional appearance (and so should you be), and as a speaker, professional networking coach, and events organizer, I have to have that professional appearance at all times. Dressing business casual is not bad, but if you can afford wearing a suit every now and then, it adds an extra level of professionalism. Now, do I wear a suit to the grocery store? No, but if I just happen to go there after a networking event, then I will be seen with a suit on. On weekends and at non-professional events, I can be seen dressed casually.

So, how do you dress for networking? Great question. Dress for the occasion and the environment. Remember, networking is like fishing. Every networking environment is different, so you want to be sure to dress for the event that you will be attending. If you know the event is going to be outside and the temperature will be 85 degrees, it's probably better to be more business casual versus wearing a wool three-piece suit with a tie! Your appearance is the first thing a person sees when they encounter you, so you want to make sure your professional 'brand' is on display.

Your attitude and actions are also part of your appearance and your 'brand', so you will need to make sure they're in order when you step out as well. It doesn't matter how nice your suit, dress, shoes, purse, etc. is if you have a BAD attitude. If you have a bad day (and ALL of us have them from time to time) and you feel like your mood and attitude is not the best, DO NOT GO OUT AND NETWORK! Unfortunately, in the scenario where your job forces you to go on a day/time, you have no choice. If that is the case, I encourage you to try to keep a smile on your face and the conversations brief, so you can get through the event. You can make up for it in the follow-up and in the future meetings.

Let's say you are attending a chamber event and you meet someone for the very first time. Here is how you would take someone through the 'YOU' channel:

1. SMILE, shake hands, and introduce yourself

While this is the OBVIOUS thing to do, it is unfortunately a lost act. Some folks get so focused on 'getting the deal' that they forget to do this. This is also the way to begin to break down the walls of distrust. If a person doesn't trust you, they won't buy from you, work with you, or hire you, so the smile and shaking hands starts to show you can be trustworthy. Your smile and handshake also transfers your positive energy to the person you are meeting. If the person was having a bad day, I can guarantee that your smile and handshake will change the person's mindset and feelings about the day.

2. Start to ask questions based on the acronym F.O.R.M. (Family, Occupation, Recreation, Motivation)

If you have a sales background, you may be familiar with the F.O.R.M. acronym, as I know it is taught within numerous companies and organizations. F.O.R.M. is important, as it gets the person talking about the thing they know best: themselves! We love to talk about ourselves and what is going on with us, so when you get someone to talk about their family, what they do for a living, what they do for fun, and what motivates them, THEY ARE IN HEAVEN! Why? Most people don't get the opportunity to talk about themselves to anyone, so when given the opportunity, they will take advantage of it. F.O.R.M. also shows you more as a listener than a talker, which breaks down the walls of distrust even more. The person may begin to ask questions about you, and that is ok. Be sure to answer them, but don't fall into the trap of talking more about yourself than the other person. The key is to answer their question and get back to focusing on him/her.

When you give a person the opportunity to talk, a couple of opportunities open up for you. First, you are learning more about the person you are talking to. The more you know about a person, the better you know how to serve them. If you ask the right questions around F.O.R.M., you can even find out if now is the time that they are looking for what you are offering. Remember, it's not when YOU want them to buy your product or service or hire you, it's all about when he/she is ready to purchase/hire. Your ultimate goal should not be to find this out, but to genuinely find out more about who the person is. Another opportunity that opens up is that you may have made a new friend. While this may not be your intent in the beginning, it sometimes becomes the result of finding out you and the other person have a lot in common. At this point, be sure to ask for a business card, and give the person one of yours as well. Be sure to also take notes on what you learned from the person. Why is this important? You'll find out in steps 5 and 6.

3. Ask 'THE MAGIC QUESTION'

I know this is not a magic book, but in the years that I have been in business, there is one question that has 'magically' opened up opportunities for me and the people I talk to. It's not a complicated question, but it is a question that, when it is asked, is MOVING and POWERFUL at its core. If you have used F.O.R.M., you have probably asked a question or two around the O and M (occupation and motivation). Once you know what those two are for the person, here is the magic question to ask:

"What can I do to assist you in that endeavor?"

When you ask this question, you officially become MEMORABLE! Any distrust walls that were up are probably down. Why? Because no one else will ask this question the rest of the night (unless they've read this book or hired me as coach, of course!). Part of setting yourself apart from others is showing that you are a servant to others. The majority of the people who go to networking events are only going for themselves and what they want. It is selfish, but it is true. Since this is the case, you will set yourself apart from the rest by having a servant's mentality. To quote the great Zig Ziglar: "You will get everything that you want in life, if you help enough people get what they want." Some people may think you have a selfish motive behind wanting to help them, but that is normal. The way to get past that is to prove them wrong by giving them the help you agreed to give them. Once you prove them wrong, you will have a colleague and resource for life!

4. Set an 'appointment'
What kind of appointment? If you have asked enough questions and the person has made it CLEAR that your product/service/skill is something they need at this point and time, then your appointment will be to meet with that person to give them more information on your product/service/skill and/or have a monetary transaction for your product/service. This scenario does not happen often, so do not expect

that every time you tell someone about your product, service, or skillset they will be ready to listen, buy, and/or hire. Remember, it's all about their timing and not yours. The appointment you normally will set is to have lunch or coffee with the person to learn more about what he/she does and what resources you can send their way. If it's a businessperson, you can set the appointment to learn more about the business in order to best send referrals the person's way. There's no right or wrong way to set the appointment, but here's an example that you can follow: "Mr. Jones, it was such a pleasure to meet you and learn more about you and your endeavors. Let's schedule a lunch or some time over coffee, so I can hear more about your endeavors, so I know what resources I can send you in the future. Which day works best for you?" In all of my years of business and networking, I have yet to run across anyone who didn't want to meet with me after setting an appointment in that manner. Because you are wanting to listen to the person to learn more about them and you want to add value to them, there is no way they can tell you no. One of the questions I get from my coaching clients is this: "So, am I setting appointments with everyone I meet?!" The answer is no. Not everyone you meet will be receptive to you, your service mentality, your products/services, and/or your skillset. Remember, the purpose of networking is to serve those who want to be served, whether it is through a resource you have or your own products/services/skillsets.

5. Follow up

Remember the business card of the person you took notes on? Give the person a call within 24 to 48 hours thanking them for the meeting and reminding them of the appointment that you two set. What does this do? Simple. It reminds the person of the meeting and puts you back in the person's frame of mind. Again, this is another piece in being memorable to other people. If your business card is set up how I recommend you set it up, the person will pull it out and then make a visual reference to who you were which puts you in a more memorable light. If the person doesn't answer, go ahead and leave a voicemail with the thank you and reminder and send an email with the thank you. If your meeting with the person is not for several days, here is something that will make you more than memorable: take out a thank you card, write a thank you note telling the person you were pleased to meet him/her, and send it to the address on their business card. We have talked about the importance of being memorable to the people we meet, and if you want to take becoming memorable to the next level, do this step! We live in a time where 'snail mail' is not used as much as it used to be due to advances in technology. While 'snail mail' is not used as frequently, people still appreciate receiving cards and letters in the mail. Because of this, you will become very memorable when you send that thank you card in the mail. Here is an example of a thank you note that I have written to someone I have met while networking:

Mr. Franco,

It was a pleasure to meet you at the mixer at the Gantt center. I look forward to our meeting next week to learn more about your company.

Notice that the note is handwritten. Yes, I have bad handwriting, but despite that, the person I sent it to was very appreciative. When we had our meeting, the person enrolled in one of our legal services plans all because of the kindness that I showed. Does that happen every time? No, but I have a greater chance of it happening when I do send the card.

6. Take him/her through the other channels

After you have the first meeting with the person, the person may or may not be ready to do business with you, send you leads and referrals, and/or hire you. It's not going to be because of your product/service/skillset, what you wear, or what you said. The reason that most people put off making a transaction or giving a referral is due to timing. It could be that the person is not in a financial position to make the transaction or the person feels that they will not use your product/service right away. Regardless of what that reason is, DO NOT TAKE IT PERSONALLY! Take it from a guy who used to take it personally every time someone didn't enroll in my services or hire me to be their coach. It is NEVER about your timing; it's all about their timing.

"Well, how will I know when the person will be ready?"

There are a million ways to close a sale, so my hope is that if he/she said he/she was not ready, you asked the simple question of when the person would be ready. (If you are not familiar with how to close, feel free to visit our Facebook page and request a great closing video!) Whether or not you know the date the person will be ready to close the deal, you have to keep the person engaged with you. This is where the other networking channels come in. With the advances of social media, it allows you to stay in contact with your business contacts (and personal ones, of course) to keep them abreast of what you and your company are up to. Now there is a 'method to the madness' when it comes to these other channels, and these next few chapters will help you in setting them up and implementing them to take your contacts through.

3 SECOND CHANNEL - FACEBOOK

To date, Facebook has the most users of all of the social media platforms. Because of this, we will be starting with this widely used social media platform. Facebook is mostly used for keeping friends connected on the goings on of a person's day, but there are many professional uses for Facebook, especially in the area of professional networking. There are two types of pages that one can use on Facebook for their professional networking endeavors: the personal page and the business page. The two may sound different, but they are actually the same as they will both represent your 'brand.' One will represent your personal brand while the other page will represent your company brand.

"Does this mean I cannot be myself on my personal page?"

That's not what I am saying. I actually want you to be who are and represent who you are. I will recommend that you limit the type of personal content that you put on this page. Unless your business is a baker, caterer, or chef, I would advise you to NOT post what you cook and eat all day every day. Like me, you have probably seen this more times than you care to admit. I would also highly advise against airing ANY 'dirty laundry' or matchmaking tactics either. If Facebook is going to be a good channel to create leads and new professional relationships, you will need to be conscious about what you put out there. It's like the saying goes: 'What you put into it is what you get out of it.'

The Personal Page

Let's break down the personal page, its components, and how to use them for professional networking. I will use my page as a sample.

1. Profile picture

Your picture is the starting point for your page as it identifies who you are. Since you want your professional brand to be on display, you will want to use a nice professional headshot as your picture. I know every person's budget is different, so if all you can do is a quick headshot with your phone, that will work in the short term. As you begin to build your professional brand and reputation, I would highly recommend getting with a professional photographer to get some headshots done. As you read this book to improve your networking skills, you might want to create a professional relationship with a professional photographer and do some 'bartering' to get your headshot costs reduced.

Now, will the headshot be used all the time? Of course not. The headshot will serve as your foundational picture that will be used the majority of the time to show people who you are. You will also want to show the 'personal' sides of you, so feel free to use shots of you enjoying life. This can include pictures with you and your family, you doing a favorite hobby, or you on a favorite vacation. I would recommend rotating your pictures once a week, making sure that your headshot is the profile picture that is shown the most.

2. Cover picture

Not too long ago, Facebook added the option of creating a cover picture in conjunction with the profile picture. It's not mandatory to have a cover picture, but it allows you to get creative in telling more about yourself via a picture. The cover picture that you see on mine is a picture I took of an inspirational quote from NASCAR legend Dale Earnhardt. I was visiting the NASCAR Hall Of Fame in Charlotte, NC, and when I saw it and read it, I knew I had to capture it, as it captured the essence of my thoughts about business. When Facebook introduced the cover picture, it immediately went up as my cover picture. Maybe there's a certain image that embodies your brand or personality. If you have such an image, I would recommend using it for your cover photo to add another layer of 'personality' to your page.

3. About

This is the area of your page that describes who are as a person. Certain aspects like education, where you work, relationship status, and where you live are just a few of the items that you can inform your visitors of. Since you will be using Facebook as a channel to create and cultivate professional relationships, there are a few recommendations that I have for this part of your page:

a. Do not post ANY type of sensitive personal information (i.e. your address, your phone number) - Identity theft is at an all-time high, and it's only going to get worse. Thieves of all kinds browse social media sites to find this kind of information to find their next prey. Not putting this type of information on your page keeps you safe. If you interact with someone in this channel and get to know him/her, you can give out the personal information you are comfortable giving out at that point.

b. If you are networking for a business outside of your job, do not list your job - Employers are now going to the internet to learn not only about people who are applying for jobs but also about those who work for them. What better place to learn about a person than on a person's social media sites? Some companies frown upon 'moonlighting' or having businesses outside of their own company, so if you are employed, it's always good to not include where you work. The same goes if you have a job and are looking for new employment.

4. Timeline entries

Now, here is where we get the 'meat and potatoes' in dealing with networking via this channel. Your timeline entries are where your friends and followers interact with you. The goal for a good timeline entry is to spark a type of interaction. There are three types of interactions that one strives for with this particular channel: LIKEs, Shares, and Comments.

The LIKE is simply when someone reads your post and clicks the LIKE button beneath the post. While some people feel that this is meaningless, it is actually very meaningful, as this means that what you have posted has resonated in some way with the reader. Depending on the relationship you have with the person and what the post was about, this may mean that the person is ready to start a conversation. I'll talk more about that in detail shortly.

The person may also share the post with his/her network. The person does this by clicking the Share button below your post. This is a higher level of interaction as the post resonated with the person so much that he/she was willing to share what you said with all of the people in his/her network. In addition to your post going to more people outside of your network, there is a possibility that some of those people may friend you and become part of your network. This is also a very good sign that the person wants to start a conversation.

The highest level of interaction one can give a post is if the person makes a comment about what you post. This is a sure sign that the person wants to engage in a conversation about your post.

"Why is engagement so important?"

Good question. Engagement is what tells you what is resonating with people. If you know what is resonating with people, then you can start conversations. Those conversations lead to relationship building which can eventually lead to potential sales and leads. So, how does one get engagement? Two words: good content. Let's discuss what good content is as it will be used here and in the other channels.

Let's take a look at this post:

"I just got out of bed..."

If you saw something like this, what would you say? 'So what?' 'Who cares?' 'Go back to bed.' This post is not very engaging, and a lot of stuff that is put on Facebook and other social media is not. In order to be seen above all of the 'other' types of posts, your post has to stand out. You can actually say "I just got out of bed," but in a way that draws positive attention to it and cause engagement. There are three different types of content that you can use in your timeline: words, pictures, and videos. Just as there are differing levels of interaction, there are different levels of content that you can provide. Let's look at words first, as this is the first level of content. Let's rewrite "I just got out of bed" in a way that invokes engagement:

"Blessed and thankful to see another day, so I can bless others!"

After reading this, I am sure that it inspired you in some way, and if it came across your timeline, you would probably LIKE it, share it with your followers, and make some type of comment about it. These are the types of action that you want to invoke with your content. Now, is everyone going to like EVERYTHING that you put on your timeline? Of course not. The goal is to put out content that adds value to those who see it.

The next level of content is pictures. The saying goes 'A picture is worth a thousand words,' and that is very true when using pictures in your timeline posts. Let's take the "I just got out of bed" post and turn it into a picture:

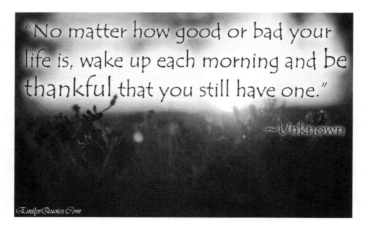

Although the picture itself has words also, the visual aspects of the picture stimulate our visual sense more than the words do. Because of this, pictures tend get more engagement (LIKEs, shares, and comments) than just words. Even the pictures of your amazing vacation can raise eyebrows and cause engagement. When you post pictures, be sure to include a descriptive comment about it along with a hashtag keyword. What is a hashtag keyword, you ask? I will describe hashtags and how they work later in the book.

The highest level of content you can post on your timeline is video. It is the highest level of content as you can have audio, video, and words to paint the picture of what you want to get across. Due to the ease of recording moments in time via smartphones and other portable recording devices, more and more people are capturing their lives and feelings via video. While it may not be a major motion picture, sharing a short video can evoke immediate emotions and cause instant engagement from your Facebook followers. While I can't place an actual video on paper, I would encourage you to visit the Stand & Deliver, LLC Facebook page, and request to view the video I created called 'Not a Resolution... A MUST!' as an example of how a video can invoke engagement. Again, it's FREE!

The Professional Page

If you are working for someone, and you are improving your networking skills for your job, feel free to skip this section, but if you are an entrepreneur or looking for another job, it is important to have a professional page set up for your business/job hunting endeavors. While your business or professional career is YOUR creation and a part of who you are, YOU and the business/career are two separate entities. Because of this, Facebook created different features for the professional page. A lot of components are the same as far as presentation and set up except you can create multiple professional pages versus only having one personal page.

For example, if you are looking for a job and have a couple of businesses on the side, you are able to create a page for your job hunting purposes as well as a page for each of the businesses. When you create a professional page, there are numerous types of pages you can create depending on your profession or industry. I recommend you look through all of the options and pick the best one for you. These pages can be made public or private. If a page is public, a person can gain access to it by simply 'liking' the page. A person gains access to a private page after he/she 'likes' a page and a page administrator approves their access. If you run a business, you can give other people in your organization access to administer content and maintain the page as long as they are on Facebook.

Regardless of if you are job hunting or promoting your business, I would recommend having a public page. This shows transparency about who you are professionally and allows easier access to the professional information that you are sharing. I would also recommend creating 'incentives' for those who 'like' and join your page. A lot of the larger companies give coupons or other types of freebies when new people 'like' their page in order to increase visits and likes to their page, so I would encourage you to do the same if you are creating a professional page for your business. Once they follow your professional page, you can create other ongoing incentives to keep them engaged with your page.

As far as content that you post goes, the same rules that I stated earlier in the chapter apply. Since these pages deal more with your professional side, I would limit how much personal content you put on these pages. I recommended earlier to have a professional mindset dealing with your personal page, but these pages are where you want to strictly put your professional content. Because this is your professional page, you can post employer recommendations and customer recommendations, as well as insightful articles on your product, service, and/or industry. Although you are posting professional content, I would advise against constantly putting 'sales pitches' out on your professional page. Again, professional networking is all about creating and maintaining relationships, so be sure that your content adds value to the people following your page. If your content does not add value, you can lose your followers' engagement as well as have people 'unfollow' your page. If you stick to the service mentality with your content, your page will have more engaged followers.

4 THIRD CHANNEL - TWITTER

While Facebook may have the most users, Twitter is definitely a close second. While both are great channels in the multi-channel system, they are different in function, purpose, and following. Twitter's core purpose is sending short but timely updates. Twitter only allows 140 characters per message in its timeline. Think of it as sending a text message to everyone in your phone. Although Twitter's core is quick and timely messages, it still has relational and conversation functions that allow for engagement like Facebook does.

"Well, if Facebook and Twitter are somewhat the same, why do I need to have both?"

I as well as many social media gurus get that question a lot. The simplest reason is this: Some just like Facebook, and some just like Twitter. You would be surprised at the number of people who will use one and not the other. Depending on what they are using it for, it's probably ok, but if they are in business for themselves or working in some type of sales/marketing profession, they are losing out on some key market share and demographics. Since we are talking about the Multi-Channel Networking System, you are missing a cog in the wheel of engagement if you pick one over the other. It is because of this that I encourage you to learn this and all of the components of the system. Let's look at the components of Twitter, and their purpose for this channel. I will use my Twitter account as an example:

1. Twitter Handle

Your Twitter handle is your 'username' for Twitter, but more importantly, it's how people will identify you on Twitter. One of my favorite movies of all time is Smokey and the Bandit. For those who are not familiar with the movie and/or are too young to even know the movie, Smokey and the Bandit is about two truckers trying to 'bootleg' alcohol from Texas to Georgia as part of a bet made by a father and son. The best parts of the movie are when the truckers are communicating over the CB radios as they try to help 'The Bandit' and 'The Snowman' achieve their goal. Yes, those were their CB radio names or 'handles' as they are called. Call their names catchy or stupid, they had purpose and told the other CB radio users who they were and what they were about. Twitter is no different. When you are using this channel, people need to know a little about who you are based on your name, so they know whether or not they should follow you.

"Can I use my name or parts of my own name?"

Yes, but unless your name is Oprah, LeBron James, or Sir Richard Branson, it is a good idea to create a catchy name to let people know who you are until your name becomes a household name.

"What name should I choose?"

First off, your name can only be 15 characters, so if you want to be called @TheBestThatEverLived, it's not happening. You will want your name to be centered around your personal brand. I would recommend revisiting the branding workshop to see what words describe you and your brand and let that develop into your Twitter name. I came up with @mrresourcemogul in the same way. I took a good look at my brand, and I saw that I was all about giving out resources in my community, hence came the name.

There are millions of Twitter users out there, so the name that you may be thinking of may already be in use. Since this is the case, it is always a good idea to come up with two or three alternatives just in case the one you first thought of is already taken.

It's also good to be open to evolve your Twitter name as your brand evolves. @MrResourceMogul wasn't always my Twitter name. My first Twitter name was actually a website that I created for another business, but as I became more of a resource driver, I changed my name to suit where I was in business. This is an integral part of setting this channel up, but I do encourage you to be creative and have fun with it. Now, if you're using Twitter to assist with your job or getting a new job, using your name will probably be a safe bet.

2. Picture

Just like Facebook, your picture is how prospective followers will 'see' you. Facebook and Twitter are similar in that you want to make sure the picture you select matches the 'brand' that you set up. For example, if the Twitter account you are setting up is yours to assist with the sales that you do for your company, it is a good idea to use a professional headshot as your picture. If the account is for your business, it's a good idea to have your company logo as the picture. My Twitter account is a hybrid as it deals with both my business and me as a personal brand. Because of this, I used one of my headshots for my picture instead of using my Stand & Deliver logo. There is no 'right or wrong' in the selection of the picture as long as the picture professionally represents you and the brand you want to showcase online.

3. Banner

The banner picture is just like the banner picture on Facebook. It allows for an added picture to describe you and your brand. Just as in the selection of your profile picture, you will want to be strategic and selective based on the brand you are wanting to showcase. For example, if you are using your business logo as your profile picture, it may be a good idea to have a picture of you and your business team as the banner picture. If your profile picture is your headshot, you may want a photo of a favorite quote or activity associated with your brand. Just like on Facebook, this is a creative, fun way to add some description about who you are and what your brand is.

4. Location

Like any social media, you do not want to put your home address for your location. Instead, make it as general as the city that you live in. If your job or business is one that goes outside of your city, you may want to include the other cities, states, and countries that you frequent. This gives the person an idea of where you are and where you frequent.

5. Bio

Just like a Twitter message, your bio has to be quick and to the point. As much as you want to give your life story from Kindergarten up to this point, it's not going to happen. Think of your bio as your 'elevator speech' for who you are. When we talked about elevator speeches earlier, we mention that they had to be quick and invoke curiosity. Your Twitter bio has to do the same thing. Take a look at my Twitter bio:

Professional speaker; professional networking coach; entrepreneur; mentor; AΦA. Changing the world one person at a time. Support the crusade!

While it may not encompass everything that I do, it offers just enough information while the 'Support the crusade' statement evokes the curiosity to ask, "What crusade?"

6. Timeline and Direct Messages

Like Facebook, your timeline messages or 'tweets' as they are called have to have great substance and content in order to start engagement with one or some of your 'followers.' As I stated earlier, your message can only be 140 characters in length. Due to this limit, your message has to pack a lot of punch in a small amount of words. The good thing about Twitter is that it can use pictures and videos in the same way Facebook does. Since this is the case, the same engagement rules that I spoke of in the Facebook chapter apply here. The more you use pictures and video, the more likely it will be for someone to engage with you.

Now, Twitter does have a conversation component like Facebook. If a follower of yours wants to comment on your entry, your follower would simply reply to you. The cool thing about that is when a follower replies to you, your Twitter handle shows up in the follower's timeline. This means that the follower's followers can see your handle, potentially reach out to you, and follow you! (Follow me?)

Like Facebook, Twitter has a 'LIKE' function, but in Twitter there are two ways to 'like' a message. One way is to make a message a favorite message. If a follower likes your post, the follower can mark it as a favorite and the follower can reference it at a later time. There is also a 'retweet' function. If a follower likes your post, the follower resends or 'retweets' your exact message out to his or her followers. It's much like the reply except it's your message that is getting sent out to the follower's followers. The retweet is a higher level of engagement than a favorite as the retweet shares the message while the favorite does not.

Twitter's advantage over Facebook is that you can grow a network outside of your own fairly quickly if you are posting great content and your followers are retweeting to their networks. Because Twitter is more fast-paced due to the length of messages sent, you will have to post more often on Twitter than on Facebook as timeline messages can scroll off faster than on Facebook. Although this is the case, make sure you are not 'tweeting just to be tweeting.' You want to make sure that your messages are timely, but engaging to your followers.

"So, when do I post?"

Great question. I will be discussing not only when to post to Twitter but also when to post to the other channels in a later chapter. Just like Facebook, you also want to make sure that you are using hashtags, so your tweets can be found by someone that may be searching for the topics that you are speaking on.

"What do you mean by search?"

I'll speak on that shortly. Now, let's discuss your followers and following. While Facebook and Twitter are both relational, Facebook deals more in who you are connected with (high school classmates, who you grew up with, etc.) than Twitter does. On Twitter it is common for someone who you have never met before who lives in another country request to follow you because what you tweeted resonated with them. It's not that common for something like this to happen on Facebook, as the person who wants to connect with you has to have some connection with another person who knows you. Twitter does have the option to make a person's 'tweets' private to those who follow them. Unless you plan on posting your company's business secrets, I would advise keeping your posts public as to make it easier for those to connect with you on this channel. In order to make the right connections, you have to be willing to be a bit transparent. Because Twitter is very open to people following one another, it is important to watch who you follow, as it is a reflection of who you are as a person. In talking with HR personnel and business owners, they always look at who a person follows in addition to their posts to get an idea of who they are.

Let's say I pull up your "following" list, and I see that you follow LeBron James, Kevin Durant, the NBA, ESPN, the Miami Heat, and Michael Jordan. From these, I can make the safe assumption that you are really into basketball and that might be one of your interests or hobbies. If you follow Rachel Ray, Guy Fieri, and the Cooking Channel, I can assume you are a chef or you love to cook. Based on your likes and interests, I assume you are following the people and 'brands' who fall in line with those likes and interests, but I will warn and recommend to have a balance as to who you follow. If you have a lot of interests that fall outside of your professional and career endeavors, I would recommend creating a special Twitter handle just for those interests as you don't want to mix business with personal too much.

Now, there is nothing wrong with having a little 'crossover' in who you follow in your account. Since my Twitter account is mostly for my business, I follow a lot of my mentors, professional colleagues, and those who I feel give great business and motivational messages. I also follow NBA star Kevin Durant, TV/radio show host Steve Harvey, and a few other celebrities who I feel give good messages throughout the day.

If you have had your Twitter account for a while, I would do an inventory of who you are following and see what 'impression' of you it is giving off. To take this a step further, have a business colleague take a look at who you follow and have him or her let you know their perception of you based on your followers. This is an important part of making sure this channel is in line with your brand, so do not take this area of your Twitter account for granted.

Twitter Search

One of the most powerful components of Twitter is the search function found at the top right hand corner of the Twitter account:

As we have discussed throughout the entire book, great professional networking is all about engagement and serving others. One of the best ways to gain engagement in this networking channel is to start engagement with other Twitter users. This is where the search function comes in handy. You can use the search function to find certain people who you may know on Twitter, but its most powerful function is to search out words and hashtags.

Let's say you were an attorney, and you were looking for those who recently got a divorce or a traffic ticket. If you put the words 'divorce' or 'traffic ticket' in the search window, it would return every tweet that contained the words divorce or traffic ticket! To take it a step further, you can do an advanced search to find those people who live in your vicinity.

While this is a powerful tool to seek those who you can help and inspire, do not do what the majority of the people do with this function. First off, do not seek out people just to 'follow them' so they ultimately follow you in return. Also, do not lead with your product or service as the 'solution' to their problem as this will immediately put you in the 'salesperson' zone.

The same rules of engagement we talked about earlier in this book when you are out and about apply online as well. You want to have a service mindset when approaching people, so when you are seeking out others, make sure you are offering help without wanting anything in return. By doing this, you will be seen as a resource and servant, and not as reaching out for your own purposes. When searching a topic and seeing the discussions on it, add value for the person by offering tips and help that can benefit the person. Letting the person know you have been in the same scenario or that you can relate to their situation can help break down the trust walls. As the conversation progresses, you can even use the F.O.R.M. method I discussed earlier to further the conversation and develop a relationship!

Whether online or offline, relationships take time to develop. Just because the person decides to follow you doesn't mean that your work is done. That is when the real work begins with you engaging with the person with your own content and you reviewing their posts for you to add value to them.

5 FOURTH CHANNEL - LINKEDIN

When it comes to online professional social media networking, no site does it better than LinkedIn. Whether you are employed or an entrepreneur, this channel is where professionals go to connect to find new opportunities. LinkedIn is a corporate recruiter's best friend as recruiters review and use LinkedIn profiles to find professionals to interview for their open positions. Like the other channels, feel free to connect with me here. Be sure to let me know that the reason you are connecting with me is because you are reading this book or I may decline your invitation not knowing what your true intentions are. Yes, there is a protocol to asking someone to connect with you on LinkedIn, and I will go over that later in this chapter. For now, let's concentrate on setting up your profile.

Let's start with your picture. The rules for using the right picture are no different here than from the other channels, so I won't spend too much time going over this. Like the other channels, a good rule of thumb is to use a professional headshot to represent who you are. Because LinkedIn is viewed more as a professional social media site than a personal one, I would advise against using any pictures that do not showcase you in a professional light, especially if you are networking for new employment.

The next component seen in a LinkedIn profile is a headline. Think of the headline as the 'attention getter' or 'elevator speech' dealing with who you are. In a few words you want to give the best description possible about who you are and what you do. Don't worry about details here, as the sections below your picture and heading will go into who you are in more detail. Remember the branding exercise we did earlier? Be sure that your headline falls in line with your brand and what you are trying to achieve.

In this section, you will also fill out your location and industry. This is important as this is how people will find you and connect with you based on where you live and what you do. If you are in the real estate industry and you live in Cleveland, OH, it is very likely that those who are in the industry and live in that area will reach out and want to connect with you. The old saying goes, "Birds of a feather, flock together." There is also a chance that someone who is looking for your services within your industry will want to reach out to you as well, so it's very important that you have where you live and your industry in this section of the profile.

These next sections are what make LinkedIn unique compared to the other networking channels within the system, so I will go into detail on their purpose and how they should be set up. To assist you in setting these sections up, it will be a good idea to break out the latest version of your résumé.

Background

Now, I don't know the last time you updated your résumé (if you are wiping dust and cobwebs off, then you need to update it ASAP!), but a lot of résumés include a summary of a person's skills and what they are wanting to achieve job wise. I would also list what skills you had as well as what you are looking for in your career endeavors. The key here is to make the reader want to scroll down to learn more about what you do, so you want to describe your skillset and endeavors in a clear and concise manner. Will EVERYONE want to take a 'deep dive' into your profile? Of course not, but the better you write out the summary, the better the chance of those you are trying to reach will look deeper into your profile. If what you say entices someone enough to look further down your profile, the next section they will run into is your experience.

This section is no different from where you would put your job experience on a résumé. The only difference is the type of content you can put here. Of course, you can use text here, and you want that to be the basis of what you use to describe your experience. Again, this is just like a résumé, so follow the same rules as you would for putting experience down on your résumé. Be sure to select the experience most relevant to what you want people to know about. If you are a hard worker, you have probably worked a lot of jobs. Nowadays, people have multiple part time jobs, part time businesses, and volunteer opportunities that have helped them gain the necessary skills needed for their career. If you fall into this category, you want to only put the jobs and experience that coincide with what you want people to know you for. For example, if you are an attorney, you would want to list the law firms and companies you have worked for, but you would not have to include the shoe store job you worked after you got out of law school. If you are networking for a job, you will definitely want to keep the experience you list close to the job or jobs you want to be hired for. If you are networking to gain more leads and exposure for your business, it's ok to add experiences outside of the business to show that you are well rounded and have interests outside of your business. Like a résumé, make sure the dates of your experience are accurate, so people can see how long you stayed in each role. One aspect that makes LinkedIn an "enhanced résumé" is the ability to add different media content to each job/experience listing. For example, if you are a personal trainer, you can attach a video of one of your training sessions to your personal training experience listing. If you have experience as a radio show host, you can attach a copy of one of your radio shows to your radio show experience listing. Here is where you can find the section to add content to your job/experience, and it is as simple as selecting the content you want and attaching it to your profile:

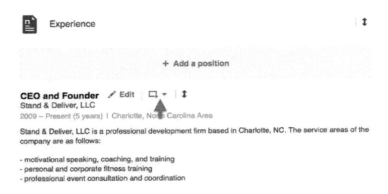

We are in an age where information and data is king, and the more evidence you can give about your abilities, the easier it is to create and sustain new opportunities for yourself. Professionals, especially those that are recruiters for companies, know and see the value that LinkedIn brings as it allows them to see past a person's résumé and see true, first hand evidence of their skillset. As you are writing out each of your jobs and roles, think about any audio, video, and/or presentations that you can add to the listing to add more depth and detail to your skillset. If you are still in the role, and you do not have any content that you can attach, I would strongly recommend that you begin collecting any and all content around your role that you can add to your LinkedIn profile. Another aspect that makes LinkedIn an "enhanced résumé " is the ability to have individuals post recommendations of your skills on your behalf. With traditional résumés, you would list the two to three people that would recommend you for the work that you do. This would be quite a drawn out process as the recruiter would then have to call the person that you listed and have a talk over the phone about your skills and experience. LinkedIn now saves a person time in having to get those recommendations as they can be listed on a person's LinkedIn profile. Now, there are a lot of different ways to request a recommendation from someone, and just because you ask someone to write you a recommendation, doesn't mean that he/she will write one for you. As we have talked about numerous times in this book, it's all about the relationships you cultivate with someone. You have a better chance of someone writing a recommendation for you that you have served or helped versus someone you just randomly sent a recommendation request to. Let's look at the general template that LinkedIn allows a person to use to request a recommendation:

I'm writing to ask if you would write a brief recommendation of my work that I can include on my LinkedIn profile. If you have any questions, please let me know.

Thanks in advance for your help.

Since this is the standard that all LinkedIn members can use to request a recommendation, it is a good idea to NOT use every word in this template. Why? As I have stated before, you want to set yourself apart from others and show your value. I don't know how many emails I get asking me for a recommendation from a person that uses this template. While I don't mind writing recommendations to those who have done good work, it would be nice to know what I am recommending them for! When I get recommendation requests using the LinkedIn template, it makes me feel that they are just sending out a mass message to those in their LinkedIn network with the hopes that one or two write one. To me, this shows no effort or thought in the request. Here's an example of what I write when I am requesting a recommendation:

Thank you so much for attending my seminar! I pray that my presentation gave you some inspiration.

Would you mind writing a brief recommendation of my talk that I can include in my LinkedIn profile? If there's anything I can do to assist you in your endeavors, please let me know. Thanks in advance for helping me out.

With me being a speaker, coach, and trainer, I ask my clients if they wouldn't mind writing a request on LinkedIn for my service. I also do the same with the attendees that I may meet after a speaking engagement. I do my best to request a recommendation as soon as I complete an engagement or training session. This way, I am fresh on their mind, and they can write a good recommendation based on what they just saw. If we are not already connected on LinkedIn, I, of course, let them know I'll be sending him or her a LinkedIn request so the recommendation can be written. I'll be talking about the process of requesting a LinkedIn connection later in this chapter.

The Rest of Your Profile

We have gone over the major points of your LinkedIn profile, but there are other aspects that are important even though they may not be at the top of the profile. Below your experience is an area for skills and endorsements. Here is what mine looks like:

Skills

Top Skills

81 Entrepreneurship	
46 Training	
38 Small Business	
37 Leadership	
36 Public Speaking	
25 Marketing	
24 Motivational Speaking	
23 Team Building	
19 Coaching	
14 Start-ups	

When you pull up your LinkedIn profile, you will sometimes be asked whether or not a LinkedIn connection of yours possesses a particular skill. If you answer 'yes' to that question, that endorsement ends up in their skills and endorsements section. I would recommend that when those boxes pop up, you take the time to answer and assist your LinkedIn connections in gaining those needed skill endorsements. Why? If someone has seen that you recommended them for a skill, they will more than likely take time out of their schedule to do the same for you. Again, it's not about what others can do for you; it's all about what you can do for others. Your endorsement could mean the difference in one of your LinkedIn colleagues getting a job or not getting a job.

There is also an Additional Info section that lists the following: Interests, Advice For Contacting, Honors & Awards and Organizations. While each of these are important to fill out, the most important are the Interests and Organizations. These two areas are the most important because your profile can be found via a LinkedIn search with one of your interests and/or organizations being a keyword. When you place an interest or your organizations in these sections, it is highlighted as a hyperlink, so when someone clicks on it, it will bring up other LinkedIn members who have put that interest or organization in their own profile. This will allow you and other LinkedIn members to find people who have common interests and who are a part of the same organization for networking purposes. As we have discussed, use these searches as ways to start a potential business relationship and not to promote you and your products/services/skills.

Connections

Just like the other social media platforms, who you are connected with is an important thing when using LinkedIn. The difference between LinkedIn and the other platforms is that LinkedIn is a bit stricter in who you can search out and connect with. With Facebook, you can send a friend request to anyone, and with Twitter, you can follow anyone and anyone can follow you (unless you have the permissions function set). Earlier in this chapter we talked about how to fill out your profile, and based on what you filled in (i.e. where you went to school, where you worked, etc.), you will be given connection suggestions by LinkedIn. Other LinkedIn members will get the same suggestions which will assist others in finding you. While this makes making connections very easy, it does not mean that the rules of engagement for professional networking are thrown out the door. With LinkedIn being a more professional social media platform than its counterparts, it is essential to apply those rules of engagement here. If you want to connect with someone on LinkedIn, you will need to send a connection request. When you send a request, LinkedIn supplies a generic request form that looks something like this:

Hi Carlos V.,

I'd like to connect with you on LinkedIn.

Just like in requesting a recommendation for your experience, it is not a good idea to use the sample requests that the site gives. As I stated before, everyone else uses the sample requests, and if you are going to set yourself apart in your networking efforts, you should take the extra time to personalize each request. The only exception I would make with this is with someone you spend a lot of time with already. This includes close friends, relatives, and coworkers who you interact with on a consistent basis. Outside of that, it's best to send a personalized message to someone you want to make a LinkedIn connection with. Here is an example of one that I have used with someone I met at a networking function:

Hi, Mr. Jones!

It was such a pleasure to meet you at the chamber event last night! It was great to learn about your accounting business, and I look forward to working with you in your professional endeavors. So that we can continue to connect, I am requesting to connect with you on LinkedIn. If there's anything I can do for you in the meantime, please let me know.

Notice that it is very personalized, it reminds the person of who I am, and it contains some of what we talked about. If I had sent this person one of the sample request messages, the person might not remember who I am and ignore my request. The purpose is to help the person remember who you are so a connection can be made.

Groups

The final component of LinkedIn we will discuss is the ability to be a part of LinkedIn Groups. LinkedIn Groups are no different than offline groups you join, as they are set up to bring professionals together with the same interests and/or background. On the home page of LinkedIn, you will see the word Interests at the top of the screen. When you highlight it, it shows the following: Companies, Groups, Pulse, Education. While the other links are valuable, we will focus on Groups as it benefits your professional networking more than the others.

When you bring it up, you can put an interest in the search box (it will say Search groups...), and it will find every group associated with that interest. If you find a group that you want to join, you may have to gain permission from the organizer to join it, as it may be a private group. The majority of the groups are not private, but due to the content that is being shared, some organizers may deem their group to be private and require permission in order for a person to become part of the group.

Once you become a member of a group, you can add value to the group by participating in the various discussions that take place or by creating your own. Remember, the goal is not be part of a group in order to sell your product of service. While you may want that result, posting information about you and how great your product and/or service is will not get you anywhere. The servant mindset comes into play here as well, so see where you can add value to the members of the group before trying to gain any value for yourself. Like we have talked about over and over, if you are not willing to look out for others before yourself, your networking will not be as effective as it could be.

While you can spend a lot of time and create some great opportunities in the groups, it is still important to create opportunities to meet 'offline.' If you find yourself having great dialogue with a colleague about a post or idea and that person lives in your vicinity, feel free to invite the person to lunch or to meet over a cup of coffee to further the discussion in person. If you all have built up enough rapport (I hope you have been using F.O.R.M. from one of the past chapters to do so!), he/she may accept your invitation. If the person doesn't accept, do not take it personally. This just means you need to develop the relationship more in order for the person to accept in the future.

In addition to finding groups that are associated with your interests, you have the option of creating your own group centered around a particular interest. For example, if you are a graphic designer, and you want to create a group of other graphic designers in your area to share professional opportunities, this would be a great way to do so. I would only recommend creating a group if you have the time to maintain it and cultivate it. Do not create a group just so people can join it and you feed off their resources. Creating and leading a group can pay some big dividends for your networking, but it will take a great deal of time and responsibility to put it together and make sure it works.

6 PUTTING IT ALL TOGETHER!

We have discussed each of channels and how to set them all up. Now it's time to put them to work! While it takes work to set the system up, there is still more work to do in order for the system to work. I will be explaining some things to help leverage your time with this system, but this does not mean the entire system is on 'auto pilot.' The word networking has the word 'work' right in the middle of it, so there will still be some work on your part to make sure the system runs smoothly.

As you and your brand are the engine that runs the system, you will need to be sure that you are out and about in your community networking and SERVING others. The word serving is in caps for reason. True networking is all about service. No matter how big or small your city is, there is always some type of networking event going on. A good place to start is with your local chamber of commerce, as they have regular events that they put on monthly and sometimes weekly. I would also recommend going to www.eventbrite.com and www.meetup.com and doing a search for professional networking events that are happening in your area. These two sites are the sites of choice for event planners to promote their events, so they will have information on networking events happening in your area.

"What events do I attend?"

I would recommend any event that is in line with your networking goals. For example, if you are networking to find a job, chamber events and after work mixers would be your best bet. If you are an entrepreneur, these same events as well as business expos would be good events to attend. After you attend an event for the first time, it is a good idea to track the effectiveness of the event. Even though you follow the rules of engagement laid out in the beginning chapters, not all events will be great events for your networking efforts. The best indicator on how well the event went is how many good professional relationships you started. A lot of people think the number of business cards one collects is the best indicator, but that is not the case. You can collect 100 business cards in one night, and not have a connection to anyone of them. This is why it is important to keep track of the effectiveness of the events you go to, especially ones that are recurring.

As you begin engaging with others and having them go through the different channels, you will need to be sure you are putting out content in each of the channels to create and cultivate the engagement of those in your network. With all of the channels within the system, one may think this is a daunting and time-wasting task. This is not the case. There are numerous social media management apps and sites on the market that can make posting your content very manageable. I recommend using Hootsuite.

Hootsuite is my app of choice as it allows me to do numerous things to make my social media management efficient. First, it allows me to schedule my posts. This means I don't have to do a 'live' post every time. To get the most effective engagement, you will need to post at the time most folks are using social media, so you can schedule your posts during these times.

"You mean, I can't just post at any time?"

You can, but if you want to maximize the viewing of your posts, you need to make sure you post at the time they are most likely to be read. Just like there are prime times to air commercials on TV and radio, there are prime times to post on social media. Because each social medium is different and when people use them are different, the time to post on each will be different. Extensive research has been done on the best times to post, so here is an estimate on the best times to post on each social network per fannit.com internet marketing:

Facebook Fast Facts:
- 751 million people use Facebook mobile
- 80% of mobile users check their phones early each morning
- People are not likely to check Facebook during work hours
- Facebook Insights reveal the best times to address your audience

best times: weekdays 6-8am, 2-5pm
worst times: all weekends, 10pm-4am

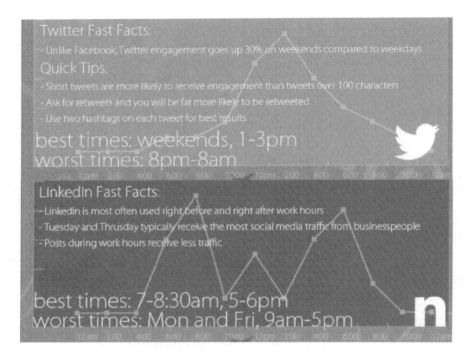

Keep in mind there is no 'perfect' schedule as to when and how often to post content. Although there are studies on when people view their social media, there will be people in your network who will not follow the same schedule due to their current state in their careers and their daily activities.

Despite the unpredictable nature of when your network looks at their social media, you can always count on individuals accessing their social media during major television and sporting events. People love to give commentary on what they are watching, and with the growth of social media, people go to Facebook and Twitter to voice their thoughts as well as give updates on what is happening on the show. The ABC network TV show Scandal is a perfect example of people flocking to Twitter and Facebook to talk about the show. The show generates an estimate of about 350,000 tweets per episode! With the show setting the stage for other shows encouraging audience engagement via social media, I would recommend having some of your social media engagement happen around a major TV event. Depending on the show or TV event, you will want your engagement to mirror or match the show. For example, I do a lot inspirational or motivational posts during sporting events like the NBA playoff games or the Super Bowl. Do I make comments about the game? Of course, I do, but I don't make that the focus of what I post.

Second reason I use Hootsuite is that you can access all of your social media accounts from Hootsuite on any device (i.e. PC, smartphone, etc.). While it is best to post at the 'prime' times of each channel, there is nothing wrong with posting when you are inspired to do so. Inspiration can come at any time, so if you are out with your smartphone and you feel inspired and you believe that your post will contribute to others, BY ALL MEANS POST!

As I stated in the channel chapters, your posts need to cause engagement and not be about selling a product or service. I mentioned using hashtags in previous chapters. A hashtag (#) is a word or collection of words that describes a social post that puts the post in a searchable category.

"Why is using hashtags important?"

When people want to find a particular subject within a post (i.e. words, video, picture), they do a search within their particular social media channel. The use of the hashtag makes the post easier to find. When the hashtag gets used often it becomes a trending topic. When a hashtag becomes a trending topic, posters will begin associating their posts with that particular topic. Anyone can create a hashtag, and a lot of companies create them as part of their branding strategy. For example, Under Armor uses the hashtag #IWill, and Gatorade uses the hashtag #WinFromWithin. Anytime anyone uses either of these hashtags, Under Armor and Gatorade can know that their product is being talked about on social media.

Twitter uses hashtags the most, but they can be used in any of the channels to begin a trending topic with your audience. Will every hashtag you create trend? Of course not. As you have discovered your brand in a previous chapter, I encourage you to create your own hashtags that align with your brand as well as use current trending hashtags to associate with your posts. You can always find out what hashtags are trending when you log into Twitter and look to the left hand side of your timeline. These same trending hashtags can be used in posts in the other channels as well. Using trending hashtags will allow your posts to appear in more searches which allows you and your brand to be found by more people on social media.

In addition to keeping track and monitoring when you post and having good hashtags, you will need to monitor how effective your postings are and on which channels. I taught in each of the channel chapters how engagement is shown in each, so you will need to monitor how effective each type of post is in each channel. You can make the same post in all of the channels, but it can end up being effective on only one and only at a certain time. To make the most out of what you post, you will need to monitor and keep statistics on your engagement for each channel. This can be a mundane task, but it is important to do in order to make sure you are posting information that causes the greatest amount of engagement. Depending on your budget, you can hire someone to do this type of analytics for you. Sites like thumbtack.com and elance.com are good resources to find someone to do analytics for you at a low cost. You can also look to hire a local college student to do this as well. If you decide to use Hootsuite to do your postings, it has analytic reports for a fee. Regardless of what method you use to monitor your posts, the information on your engagement will not only tell you how your posts are currently working, but it will give an idea of how you can improve your posts going forward to gain more engagement. For example, if your research is telling you that the posts with pictures on Facebook are gaining more engagement than posts with pictures on Twitter, then it's a good indicator to do less picture posts on Twitter and do more with words.

While this system will improve your professional networking skills, it is up to you to evolve as well. As we stated in the beginning, the system does not make you; YOU make the system. It's one thing to read this book and take the information in, but it's another to implement the information. I am living proof that the information presented in this book works. Otherwise, I wouldn't I have written it! The only way you can know if it will work for you is if you implement the information for yourself. If someone told me when I was younger that I would have been an on air radio personality, a networking coach, author, speaker, and fitness trainer all before the age of 40, I would have called him/her crazy. I owe it all to God and networking!

If you have not already done so, go through each exercise in this book, set up your channels, and put the system to work. It is important to keep track of how well the system is working, but it is more important to keep track of you and how your brand is working. Again, I am honored and privileged that you decided to purchase this book, but there are other books and trainings out there to improve you and your professional skills. Networking is the most overlooked skill in one's professional career, but there are other skills that a professional should continue to improve. I would encourage you to look at other aspects of your professional development and find resources to improve them. As stated over and over in the book, professional networking is simply service to your fellow man.

While I may not reside where you live, I want to continue to be a service to you even outside of this book. Please connect with me on all of my channels if you haven't already done so. This will keep you posted on where I am and when I will be in your area. You can also connect with me on my company website: http://www.istandanddeliver.com. Please feel free to engage with me to let me know how I can be of assistance and to ask any questions you may have about networking. Whatever resources I have are yours, so please engage with me and let me know how your networking is going. I leave you with this quote. Success is not you getting to your destination; true success is you helping as many people as you can get to their destination before you get to yours. I pray increased blessings in your career and endeavors!

54034750R10037

Made in the USA
Columbia, SC
25 March 2019